Just the Two of

A play

Ros Moruzzi

Samuel French — London
www.samuelfrench-london.co.uk

ISBN 978 0 573 12144 9

CHARACTERS

Matt Kominsky, 40ish, aspiring writer
Ruth Kominsky, 40ish, nurse
Freya Harvey, 18, manipulative teenager
Karen Harvey, 40ish, her manipulated mother
Pauline, 60s, Matt's interfering mother
Bev, 40ish, Karen's ex-friend
Robin, Karen's new partner

The action takes place in the pleasant living room of Matt's and Ruth's ground floor apartment

Time—the present

COPYRIGHT INFORMATION
(See also page ii)

JUST THE TWO OF US

SCENE 1

The setting throughout is the pleasant living room of Matt's and Ruth's ground floor apartment

There is a sofa, a table and chairs. On the table is a tray set for a simple supper for two. There is also a desk with a bin and a chair next to it. On the desk are a telephone, a computer and printer. There are two interior doors, one leading to the bedroom and one to the kitchen, and a window. There is a front door with a hall area off from the living room

As the Lights come up, the printer is printing out pages of a manuscript

Matt enters from the kitchen with a mug of tea. He puts the mug on the desk. Recovering the printout he examines the title page with satisfaction, ready to read aloud

Matt Right, "The Deadly Blade," Yes, that'll grab 'em. "The Deadly Blade, by Matt Kominsky." Chapter One. Draft fifteen. (*He pauses dramatically. Reading*) "The dark, rain-spattered courtyard echoed with the terrible woman's scream." What? Oh, you moron. (*Dumping the manuscript in the bin*) Rubbish! Rubbish, rubbish, crap!

With a sigh of resignation, Matt returns to his seat at the computer

A pause

Right. Chapter One. (*He types*)

Ruth enters the hall, tired, glad to be home. She takes off her cardigan, revealing a nurse's uniform

Ruth (*calling*) Hi, love, I'm home. How's it going?

Matt (*hunched over the keyboard, shouting*) Bugger! Delete, delete, delete, delete, delete.

Ruth walks into the living room, leans over Matt's hunched frame and kisses his cheek

Ruth Oh dear. Hello, love. Hi!

Matt Oh, hi. Didn't hear you come in.

Ruth No. How's it going?

Matt Mm, not too bad. I've got the title and the ending.

Ruth That's good.

Matt It's the rest of it that's the problem.

Ruth Oh dear. Well, keep at it. I bet Shakespeare had the same trouble.

Matt No. That's it. I am calling it a day. Anyway, how are you, sweetheart?

Ruth Shattered. You've no regrets then? You know, leaving work? Not that I'm suggesting that this isn't ——

Matt Oh good Lord, no. This is much more fulfilling. Will be, anyway, I'm sure. Now sit down, your house-husband will see to your every desire.

Ruth My only desire is to get these shoes off. (*She flops down on the sofa*) Oh, bliss.

Matt Now what can I get you? (*With a French accent*) A white wine? Gin and tonic? A little cocktail perhaps, with a cherry and an umbrella?

Ruth No, I'll have a nice cup of tea. Yours'll do, you didn't drink it.

Matt It'll be lukewarm.

Ruth I don't care. It's made. It'll be fine. Then come and sit here.

Matt (*handing Ruth his mug*) Your cold tea, madam. My wife is easily pleased.

Ruth No I'm not. That's why it took me so long to find the right man.

Matt Works both ways. (*He sits next to her and puts his arm around her*) Good day, bad day?

Ruth Both. The good was the ward was given a star rating for cleanliness. But we lost another prem. this morning. Twenty-six weeker.

Matt I'm sorry.

Ruth Mm.

Matt Must be really rough. Especially with you ——

Ruth No. It's funny but you keep it, separate, somehow. If I started thinking … anyway, it wasn't meant to be. I've got my babies in the hospital. And you when I come home. Just the two of us, eh?

Matt Just the two of us. There's a lot to be said for it.

Ruth (*with a touch of sadness*) I guess.

Matt Yes. (*Pause*) Anyway, are you hungry?

Ruth I am actually. What are we having?

Matt Lasagne. In about half an hour?

Ruth Mmm. You're a saint.

Matt I know. It's a Saint Matthew's special.

Ruth I don't care if it's Saint Michael's as long as I don't have to cook it. I'll get out of these clothes. Anyone phoned?

Matt No, just a couple of cold calls. Don't know how they get our number.

Ruth Once you're on a database you've had it. They sell them on, the whole address list. Not right. Has to be some way of blocking them. What was it this time? Double glazing? Insurance? Change your gas supply?

Matt I didn't let her get that far. She even had my name. "Am I speaking to Matthew Kominski?" Yes you are, so bugger off, I told her.

Ruth Matt, that's not like you.

Matt Well, I was tempted. I just said we don't take cold calls.

Ruth I suppose they're only doing their job.

Matt I guess. Anyway, you get changed. I'll shut this down. Ah well, tomorrow is another day. (*He gets up and shuts down his computer*)

Ruth exits to the bedroom

The phone rings

> (*Calling*) I'll get it! … (*Into the phone*) Hello… (*He sighs*) Yes. Yes,
> dear, I *am* Matthew Kominski, and I know you are only doing your
> job but I have no wish to change my mobile, or my energy supply,
> or to buy anything, win anything or subscribe to anything so please
> do not call me ever, ever, ever again. Goodbye. (*He hangs up*)

Ruth enters, clothes partly changed

Ruth Not again! Have we won another holiday?

Matt I didn't let her get that far. We'll have to do something about it.

Ruth We've been saying that for months. Mmm, gorgeous smell, I'm
ravenous.

Matt Everything's on the table.

Ruth No, let's have it on our knees. We'll have a nice, quiet, lazy
evening. (*She puts the tray on the coffee table*)

Matt Sounds good. I'll open a bottle.

Matt exits to the kitchen

> (*calling, off*) Red? White?

Ruth Yes, please! Any! Bring the opener.

Matt returns with a bottle of white wine

Matt No need, a screw top. I love screw tops! Made for instant
gratification. (*He unscrews the cap*)

Ruth Two plates, two forks, two napkins, two glasses. I am looking
forward to this.

The phone rings

> Oh not again. I'll tell them this time. (*Into the phone*) Will you please
> stop calling us, we've had enough! Pauline, sorry! (*Mouthing, to Matt*)
> Your mother. (*Into the phone*) I thought it was another of those selling
> things, calls, you know, we keep getting them. Do you want Matt?

Matt pours the wine into two glasses, shaking his head, frantically

He's just here. (*She hands Matt the phone*)

Matt (*into the phone*) Hello, Mother… No, not yet, we were just about to, actually, so… Lasagne, actually… no, not Chinese, Italian. No, I did, Ruth's only just got in…Yes I know you always had a cooked dinner ready for my dad — but this is the way we… I am working. I told you, a novel. No, not published yet, you have to write it first. I'd better — What?… Yes, we are in tonight.

Ruth shakes her head

No, no need. Really… Well, not before nine, we're going to eat. And after nine we'll probably be in bed…(*He sighs*) Five past then. Okay. We'll see you later. (*He hangs up the phone*)

Ruth See you later?

Matt Sorry. I couldn't think of anything. She's just popping in with a —

Ruth Not one of her crumbles?

Matt Yup. She had a load of apples and thought we might like one.

Ruth Because her poor son doesn't have a wife who cooks him wovely puddies like she used to do. I wish she'd leave us al —

Matt I'll get rid of her, don't worry. (*He hands her a glass*)

Ruth You'd better, that's all. Nice quiet evening, I said.

Matt Come on, it's only half seven. Let's make the most of it. Cheers.

Ruth Cheers.

Matt and Ruth clink glasses and go to drink

The doorbell rings

I don't believe it. Whoever it is, get rid of them.

Clutching a wine bottle and glass, Matt goes to the window and looks out

Matt Two women. One looks younger. Quite smartly dressed.

Ruth Two? It'll be Jehovah's Witnesses. I know they mean well but you'll be there all night. Tell them we've got our own beliefs, that usually works. Catholic, Jewish, anything. I'll finish changing.

Still holding the wine bottle and glass, Matt opens the front door

Ruth exits to the bedroom

Freya, nervously excited and Karen, looking uncomfortable, are standing at the door

Matt Yes?

Karen Excuse me, but are you by any chance —— ?

Matt — Religious. Yes we are, very much so. We're, er, Muslim. *(Noting the wine)* Ex Muslims actually. Lapsed.

Karen Pardon?

Matt Didn't work out. Too fond of this stuff. So now we're Orthodox Presbyterian atheists. Yes, that's us. So, religious-wise, we're comprehensively covered. So, not today thank you. Goodbye!

Karen No! Please. That's not why we're here ——

Freya — Yeah, please! We are so, like, not religious.

Karen We're really sorry to disturb you.

Matt Don't mention it. So, if there's nothing else ——

Karen No, please. We're sure we've got the right address.

Matt Right address for whom?

Freya Is your name Matthew? Please, please, say it is.

Matt It is, yes. Matt.

Freya Ohmygod, it is! It's him, it is ——

Karen We're very sorry to disturb you like this, but she's given me no peace.

Freya I've tried calling, like, three times, and then on my mobile — it was like ——

Karen She said you seemed to think she was a call centre.

Matt Oh, was that you?

Scene 1

Freya Yes — and I am so not a call centre. I mean, it's not as though I sound, like, Indian or anything. Ohmygosh, it's you, this is so, totally —

Karen — Hold on, Freya, let's be absolutely sure.... (*Checking*) It is Matthew James Kominski?

Matt Yes. How did you get all this?

Ruth comes out of the bedroom and goes to the door

Ruth You're still here? What's going on?

Karen Sorry, we really did try to call first.

Freya This is so, totally, amazing!

Ruth What is?

Freya I can't believe, it's really him! It is him!

Ruth Good grief, she sounds like you're the Second Coming. Now we've got neighbours looking. And it's started raining. You'd better come inside. Just for a minute.

Karen Thank you.

They all go into the sitting room

Freya Ohmygod, this is so —

Karen I am sorry to just turn up like this, but she has been trying to phone you.

Freya And when you answered, you kept saying, like, "I don't need double glazing," and I was, like, so excited, thinking, like, ohmygod, that's him!

Karen I think we should introduce ourselves — and explain.

Ruth I think that's a very good idea.

Karen I'm Karen, Karen Harvey. And this is my daughter, Freya.

Freya Hi!

Ruth And...?

Karen Well, it's a bit complicated, but Freya's been doing some, tracing. Looking into her, you know, her background?

Matt What does that have to do with us?

Ruth Background? You've found some kind of link, is that what this is?

Karen That's right.

Freya Have we ever! (*She giggles*)

Ruth (*relaxing*) Ah, it's one of these ancestry things, isn't it? You know, Matt, "Who do you think you are?" People hope they're descended from Christopher Wren.

Matt — Then find they came from an Irish bog. Load of nutters if you ask me.

Ruth No, they're all doing it at the hospital.

Matt Point taken. They should be looking after patients.

Ruth No, at home, don't be silly. People do it online. (*Pause*) And I suppose there aren't that many Kominskis.

Karen (*nervously*) That's right.

Matt Are you saying you've found some connection?

Karen Yes

Matt With me?

Karen Well, yes.

Ruth So how d'you think you're connected?

Karen It's rather awkward.

Matt It can't be that awkward.

Karen Oh it is.

Matt Well?

Freya Ohmygod, this is so, like, surreal.

Ruth So, what's the relationship?

Karen Your turn, Freya. Come on.

Freya No, I can't! You tell him, Mum. Please, please! I can't now, I just so can't say it. Please.

Karen No. This was all your idea. All this.

Ruth Well?

Karen Come on.

Freya Right. This is so totally amazing. I've been, like, imagining this, like, moment, for, like, ages. And I'm really, really nervous.

Ruth So can you really, really get on with it?

Freya Ohmygod. Here we go. You're my — (*Pause, then she flings herself at Matt*) Daddy! My Daddy!

Ruth For heaven's sake, she thinks she's in *The Railway Children*.

Matt (*disentangling himself*) Please, now stop this.

Ruth Absolutely, this is ridiculous.

Freya But it's true!

Matt Let's calm down shall we? There's been a big mistake here.

Freya Oh Daddy, it is so not a mistake.

Karen It's right, we've got all the details.

Matt What details? You can't have.

Karen Well we do. I'm sorry, but we're really quite certain.

Matt This is mad.

Freya You are *so* like I imagined. Isn't he, Mummy?

Ruth If it's not a mistake it's a sick kind of joke.

Freya No, it's so not a joke! I've done all the, like, research,

Ruth (*pause*) You're serious?

Karen Absolutely.

Ruth (*glaring at Matt*) I see.

Karen I did tell her, phone first, make sure it's all right.

Freya But I tried, and you wouldn't ——

Ruth We've been through all that. Now, calmly, would somebody care to explain?

Freya I traced him!

Karen I told her not to start all this. (*To Freya*) But as usual ——

Ruth Well it looks like there's something you've failed to mention to me, Matt? Just slipped your memory, did it? Easily done.

Matt No. Absolutely not! I promise you, love, as if I wouldn't know.

Freya I was hoping it would be like, a nice surprise?

Ruth Oh we're surprised all right. Aren't we, Matt?

Matt That's an understatement.

Ruth Well this makes no sense. How old is Freya?

Freya Eighteen last January.

Karen That's when she started the trace, to find his name. I told her not to ——

Ruth So you keep saying. I don't wish to be rude but why did you need to trace her father's name? Were there that many options?

Karen No. Yes. Well in a way. It's not like it sounds.

Ruth Well it sounds very strange. If you don't mind me asking, where was she conceived?

Karen Manchester.

Ruth Manchester? That's funny, Matt, eighteen, nineteen years ago, weren't you in Manchester?

Matt Yes, doing my social work degree.

Karen Weren't you a bit ——

Matt Old? Yes, I was a mature student.

Ruth Mature in what respect, I wonder?

Matt looks perplexed

Ruth Well, Matt. I think it's time we had a contribution from you. Though it looks like you've made one already.

Matt No! Don't be ——

Ruth Well, at least it was before I knew you. So, when were you and Karen an item?

Matt
Karen } *(together)* We weren't!

Matt I've never met her before.

Ruth Oh, for heaven's sake!

Karen It's true.

Ruth Oh, so you had an Immaculate Conception did you? With that, and the Second Coming, we'll soon have the whole Bible covered. "An Immaculate Conception."

Karen Well, kind of, in a way. I went to a, clinic.

Matt reacts, the realization gradually dawning

You know, AID.

Ruth A clinic. AID. Ring any bells, Matt?

A pause

Matt Oh God. (*A pause*) I can't believe it.

Ruth We'll take that for a yes, shall we?

Matt I can't believe it.

Ruth So you said, but here we are, eighteen years later ——

Freya Me! Isn't that amazing, Matt? That makes you my bio-dad.

Ruth Bio-dad. Good grief.

A pause

Matt Unbelievable.

A pause

Freya I was hoping you'd be pleased.
Ruth Oh we are, deliriously. Aren't we, Matt?
Freya See, Mum, she is cool!
Ruth Am I? I don't know what I am. (*Curtly*) Well, under the circumstances, I ought to introduce myself. I'm Ruth, Daddy's wife. How do you do?
Karen (*awkwardly*) How do you do?
Ruth I'm cool, apparently.

A long pause

Matt Unbelievable.
Ruth Well we're going to have to sort this out.

Matt attempts to mollify Ruth. Ruth shrugs him off

Karen I'm sorry. I never wanted —— (*to Freya*) I did warn you.
Ruth No, Freya's done us all a favour.
Freya See, I knew she'd understand.
Ruth (*sarcastically*) Of *course* I do. Everything out in the open. (*To Matt*) So, something you never thought to mention?
Matt It just didn't register. (*Pause*) Are you all right?
Ruth What do you think? So how about an explanation? Daddy.
Matt I was a student.
Ruth A mature one. Supposed to be.
Matt It made no difference, I was broke. No grant, no income. And I saw this advert. Thirty quid was a lot of money then.
Freya Wow. Did you have to pay?

Matt No. Don't be so... I got thirty quid, it paid my rent.

Freya What did you have to do?

Karen Freya — we don't want to know that.

Freya I do!

Ruth And then what?

Matt Then nothing. It was supposed to be anonymous. I mean, that was the whole point. It was to help childless couples.

Freya (*admiringly*) Ah. Isn't he just so, like ——

Ruth — Stupid. So what happened to "anonymous"? (*To Freya*) How did you find all this out?

Freya I got to know this, like, social worker. And she believes it is so unfair for people not to know? And she got this like, name, from the hospital. And *she* was really brilliant. And then we got *your* name — and it was ohmygod, it must be — then I had to, you know, ring this number — and you thought I was ——

Ruth And here you are.

Karen Yes, here we are. Sorry.

Ruth So, what now?

Freya I thought we could, like, celebrate?

Ruth Well, actually Freya, call me a party pooper, but I don't quite feel like celebrating.

Freya Oh God, you don't like me.

Karen Now don't start that

Freya Nobody likes me.

Ruth It's not that, Freya, believe me. It's all this, "Daddy." It's a bit hard to take. And not — not knowing.

Matt Honestly, love, I had absolutely no idea. I really had completely forgotten about it. I mean, you didn't think of it ever being a person.

Freya It?

Matt You didn't think of anything. That was the whole point. Anonymous.

Ruth You really had forgotten?

Matt Absolutely, completely. I'm really sorry.

Freya Oh so you're sorry are you? Well I might as well not exist.

Karen Don't be silly.

Scene 1

Freya You so don't want me. Any of you. Everyone really hates me.

Karen They don't hate you. They don't know you.

Freya And never wanted to either. I am just like *so* damaged. (*She sucks her thumb*)

Ruth I suppose she's not the only one. (*To Matt*) Suddenly out of the blue, finding you've got a....

Matt I had no idea.

Ruth Well you should have. But I believe you.

Karen I'm sorry it's been such a shock. That's enough, Freya. Act your age.

Ruth Well it must be hard on her too. Here you are, have a tissue.

Matt (*to Ruth*) I'm sorry, love.

Karen I never wanted this. Really. It was Freya ——

Ruth I suppose she felt it was her right.

Freya I so needed to, like, know who I am.

Ruth Yes, that's completely understandable. Well, here we are. (*Pause. To Karen*) Would you like a drink?

Matt Yes please.

Ruth No! I meant offer one, to Karen ——

Matt Sorry. Yes, good idea. Er, white wine OK?

Freya Yes, please. Thanks, Ruth.

Matt fetches the bottle of wine

Karen No, I think maybe we should go. I'll call ——

Freya No, please, please. Look Matt's getting the wine now. Let me help!

Matt Right. Er, more glasses. We've got ours.

Matt exits to the kitchen

Ruth Yes, we were just about to have it.

Karen Oh I'm sorry.

Ruth It's all right.

Freya Ah, thanks, Ruth. I think you've been really wicked.

Ruth Wicked?

Karen It's a compliment.

Ruth (*smiling*) That's all right then. Have you had to come far?

Karen Not really, about an hour. My partner will pick us up when I call.

Ruth You never married?

Karen Oh yes. Before Freya was born.

Ruth I see.

Karen We divorced.

Ruth Anything to do with —— ?

Karen Yes, actually. We'd tried, and, 'cause he couldn't — it's hard for a man. And Freya wouldn't accept him, once she knew. They were always rowing. "You're not my Dad."

Matt returns with two glasses, still a bit bewildered

Freya Well he wasn't.

Karen Yes he was, he brought you up, he provided for you ——

Freya He was not my, like, bio-dad. Not that you'd care. (*To Ruth and Matt*) *She* wouldn't care if I never knew who I was. Too busy with *Robin*! Anyway, I didn't look like him. I look like Matt, don't I?

Ruth No.

Matt Do you think so?

Freya Yes, you are really cool looking. Isn't he, Mum?

Karen Well, yes, he is.

Freya A really fit Dad.

Matt No, I'm very out of condition.

Ruth That's not what she means.

Freya My friends will be totally green. I can't wait to tell Martine. (*To Matt*) Let me help!

Ruth (*to Karen*) Anyway, you've got a partner now, that's good.

Freya For her, maybe. Here we are. (*She hands around the glasses*) White wine for Ruth, me, Mummy. And Daddy.

Matt Thank you.

Ruth Cheers, Daddy.

Karen (*quietly*) Cheers.

Matt Cheers.

Ruth Do I need this!

A smoke alarm goes off

A pause

Karen Is something burning?
Ruth Is the oven still on?
Matt Oh no!
Ruth Oh God, what next?

Matt rushes out to the kitchen

We hear Matt cursing offstage

The alarm stops. An oven door clangs

We hear Matt cursing offstage some more

Matt returns with a blackened, smoking pan. He puts it on the table

Ruth Well done, is it?
Karen Oh that's our fault. I'm really sorry. We've ruined your meal.
Ruth Never mind. I seem to have lost my appetite.
Karen We should go.
Freya Oh, not yet! I could make you something.
Karen Don't be silly, when did you ever cook?
Freya I can do crisps. Have you got any?
Ruth Matt?
Matt There's some in the larder cupboard.
Freya Great, I'll get them!
Matt To the left of the oven.

Freya's phone rings, an absurd ringtone

Freya Mine! (*She gets her phone out and checks it*) Oh wicked, she got my message. (*Into the phone*) Hi. Hold on will you?

Karen Who is it?

Freya No one special. (*Sweetly*) Can I take this in your kitchen, please, Ruth?

Ruth Be my guest.

Freya Oh, thank you! (*She blows a kiss*)

Freya exits into the kitchen

Karen I wonder who that is?

Ruth She's very persuasive isn't she?

Karen She certainly is. (*Pause*) Would you mind if I used your loo?

Ruth Just off the bedroom, first right.

Karen takes her bag and goes out to the bedroom

Matt I don't know what to say.

Ruth Nor me.

Matt Will you forgive me?

Ruth For what?

Matt Forgetting. I honestly did. I wasn't very sober actually. I think I did it for a bet.

Ruth You'd best not let Freya know that. She is "so damaged."

Matt I hope she isn't.

Ruth I doubt it. Confused, maybe, poor girl. Difficult for Karen, too. She fancies you, you know.

Matt Nonsense.

Ruth Oh yes, she's a "D and D" — divorced and desperate.

Matt Well, I don't fancy her. (*Pause*) I'm really sorry about all this.

Ruth Behold your sins will find you out. Taken eighteen years. Not so much a sin, science. If it's medically possible, it's OK. I see it every day. Anyway… At least they're not after child support. We hope. (*Pause*) Strange, we wanted a child, and suddenly you've got one.

Matt No. Not really. Not in the… Oh Lord. Listen, we'll get rid of them as soon as possible.

Ruth A nice quiet evening. Is she still on the phone?

Matt (*listening*) I think so, yes, I can hear her.

Ruth Where's that wine? Let's have it before Karen comes back. Do I need it. Can anything else go wrong? (*She goes to drink from her wine glass*)

The doorbell rings

Matt What's the time?
Ruth Five past nine. Oh no! Your mother with her bloody crumble. That's all we need. Get rid of her. (*She goes to the front door and opens it*) Hello Pauline!

Pauline barges past her with a pudding dish wrapped in a tea towel and a carrier bag containing cream, custard and photographs

Pauline I'm not stopping long; Matt made it very clear I'm not welcome. I'll just hand this over and go. Even though I had to wait half an hour for the bus. In the pouring rain.
Matt Hey, Mum, of course you're welcome.
Ruth (*mouthing to Matt*) No she's not!
Pauline I've brought your crumble, still hot from the oven. Nearly burned my hands carrying it, but I know how you love it.
Matt Well thank you. But we do eat, you know.
Pauline (*spotting the blackened pan, then the wine*) So I see. You should keep an eye on the oven, Ruth. Especially when you've been drinking.
Ruth No, that's the way we like it, nice and black and crusty.
Matt We've had a bit of a prob ——
Pauline Well, at least you can have a proper hot sweet. I've brought cream as well, and custard. (*She puts the dish and bag on the table*) I'll get some dessert bowls shall I? If you've got any.
Ruth No, not now, please. We really don't want anything else.
Pauline I'm not surprised, if you've had that.

Ruth mouths "get rid of her" — indicating the visitors

Matt We'll have the crumble tomorrow, thanks. (*He yawns extravagantly*) We were thinking of bed actually.

Pauline I'd have thought you a bit old for that sort of thing.

Matt To sleep — not to — I've been at the computer — I really must get an early night. (*He yawns again*) Are you on earlies tomorrow, love?

Ruth Yes, I have to be up at six. (*She yawns*)

Matt We were just about to turn in.

There is the sound of a toilet flushing, then a door closing

Pauline What was that?

Matt I didn't hear anything.

Pauline There's somebody in your bedroom

Matt } (*together*) { No.

Ruth } { No there isn't.

Pauline Well, if you don't believe me, I'll go myself.

Pauline heads into the bedroom

Matt Oh Lord.

Pauline (*off*) Well excuse *me*.

Pauline returns

There is a woman in your bedroom. An attractive woman, putting lipstick on. "Just going up to bed," were we? I've read about this sort of thing, but my own son! I knew this'd happen if you married a nurse.

Ruth Oh for heaven's sake, Pauline. We've had visitors, that's all.

Pauline You never mentioned visitors when I rang. "Early night" you said. I've come all this way ——

Matt We didn't know, we weren't expecting ——

Freya bounces in with two packets of crisps

Freya Hiya!

Pauline And who's this then, may I ask?

Freya I'm Freya, hi!

Scene 2

Matt (*weakly*) Anyone like some crisps?
Freya I found two kinds. Do you want them in a bowl, Daddy?

A silence

Pauline What the heck's going on?
Ruth Maybe Daddy will explain. (*Sweetly, to Freya*) Did you make your call, dear?
Freya Yes. I so had to tell Martine about Matt, she's my best mate, she really hates her Dad and she thinks I am sooo lucky. And then I had to text Bev ——
Ruth Who's Bev?
Freya Ohmygod, don't tell Mum cause she can't stand Bev, but I had to tell her, 'cause I'd really, really promised I would and she's going to text me back. (*To Pauline*) So who are you? Ruth's Mum?
Pauline (*bewildered*) No, I am Matt's mother if you must know.
Freya Really? Oh that is so cool! Now I've got a granny as well!

Karen enters, her make-up freshened

Mum! Mum! Come and meet Granny!

Black-out

Scene 2

The same, half an hour later

Matt and Karen are sitting cosily together on the sofa, engrossed in conversation. Pauline and Freya sit beside them, sharing photos from a photo wallet. Ruth is sitting alone at the table, drinking and observing. She drains her wine, opens a new bottle and wanders to Matt and Karen to top up their glasses. They fail to look up

Ruth So sorry to interrupt.
Matt That's all right.

Karen Thanks, Ruth. (*Holding out her glass*)
Ruth (*sweetly*) Oh please don't mention it. My absolute pleasure.

Ruth returns, fed up, to the table where she sits alone, drinking and observing

Pauline Well, I would never have believed it!
Ruth You're not the only one.
Pauline If I hadn't come with Matt's crumble, I never would have known.
Ruth Some things are clearly meant to be.
Freya Can I make you some tea, Granny?
Pauline No thanks, love, you stay by your Nana. What a lovely girl, Matt. Little treasure, aren't you? Beautiful manners. She's a credit to you, Karen.
Karen Oh. Thank you.
Pauline And d'you know, the more I see her the more I can see our Matt. Oh yes, the image. Wait a minute, I've got some others here. Here we are. Who do you think that is?
Freya Is that Daddy?
Ruth Aah, Daddy!
Karen Can I see?
Pauline It certainly is. Wasn't he sweet? Ah, look, on his little potty!
Freya Aah. He is so cute.
Ruth So cute.
Pauline This is our Matt in his graduation costume. You can see the likeness there. See Karen? Wasn't he good looking?
Karen (*nodding*) He was.
Ruth Yes, very fit.
Matt So we were both in Manchester the same time?
Ruth Doesn't take a PhD to work that one out.
Matt Did you ever go to the Blue Parrot?
Karen Oh yes, and the Rexie.
Matt The Rexie? Did you know Ernie Hallows that ran it? He was a friend of mine.
Karen Ernie? I went out with his brother.
Matt John Hallows? No!

Ruth No!

Karen Yes, for about six months. Before I met Keith.

Matt Not Keith Tavener, played guitar?

Karen The very one. Do you like blues guitar?

Ruth I can't stand it myself.

Matt I love it.

Karen So do I!

Pauline Oh, you've so much in common! (*To Freya*) They make a lovely couple don't they?

Ruth (*furious*) What?

Pauline I was just saying how much they had in common. (*To Karen*) Amazing, isn't it?

Karen It really is.

Pauline You've even more in common, though, haven't you?

Matt Not sure what you mean, Mum.

Pauline Well, you know. You've had a child together, haven't you?

Silence. Matt puts his head in his hands

Ruth Bloody hell. Bloody hell! Can't you rub it in even more? As if this bloody love-in isn't enough. So you've had a child. Together. Well congratulations, you made a baby. And here she is. All I can say is, you are welcome to each other. Bloody well welcome. So why don't you just bugger off, the whole bloody lot of you.

Matt Ruthie ——

Freya I think she's upset.

Pauline I wouldn't take no notice, she always had a terrible temper.

Ruth No I have not!

Matt Come on, Ruthie.

Ruth Don't you Ruthie me, you — Don't touch me! Leave me alone! I mean it. You stay with your wonderful new, extended family!

Ruth exits to the bedroom, slamming the door

Pauline See what I mean?

Matt Ruth!

Pauline Leave her be, Matt, I would.

Karen It has been a shock for her.

Matt Listen, I'll go and er ——

Karen I think you should. Then we really must go. We've caused enough ——

A text message alert sounds on Freya's phone

Freya (*reading*) Just a minute… Oh, that's brilliant. Just need to reply. (*Texting. To Matt*) This is number 45a?

Matt Yes it is. I have to go and see Ruth.

Matt exits to the bedroom

Pauline She always was a bag of nerves.

Karen (*to Freya*) Why did you want to know the house number?

Freya Hang on … I'm trying to ——

Karen When you finish that, I want it off, my girl. It's very rude.

Pauline I don't know how they do it, do you? All those little buttons, and you can talk through them as well.

Freya And take pictures.

Pauline Isn't it marvellous?

Freya Sent.

Karen Off!

Freya (*switching her phone off*) Right. Happy now?

Pauline Have you got one of those music things where you have wires coming out of your head?

Freya An mp3 player?

Pauline I wouldn't know, but you be careful, love, I don't want my grandchild with fried brains. See this one, Freya? Remind you of anyone?

Freya Is that you in the olden days?

Pauline The fifties. Who does it remind you of?

Karen Betty Flintstone.

Freya Amy Winehouse.

Pauline No, you're the image of me, then. Like looking in a mirror.

Freya I would so love my hair like that. It's really cool.

Pauline I've always wanted a grandchild. Ruth never had one. These career girls, they leave it too late. She's probably jealous, that's what all that was about. Now listen, I've got a bit of something put away. So mind you behave yourself.

Freya That is so sweet.

Matt returns from the bedroom

Karen Is Ruth OK?

Matt I think she'll come back. Mother, that was not very tactful, to say the least.

Pauline Oh, whatever I say it's never right.

Matt Well the less said the better, in this case.

Pauline Right then, I can take a hint. I'll get my things.

Matt (*heading back to the bedroom*) Can you come, love? Mum's going.

Matt exits into the bedroom

Karen And we need to go as well. I'll call Robin to pick us up.

Freya Not yet. Please, please! Oh, Mum!

Karen That's enough of that ——

Freya But she's due any minute!

Karen Who is?

Freya (*pause*) Auntie Bev.

Karen Bev? Not Bev. You didn't tell her we were coming here?

Freya Yes. I said I'd text her if it was the right place so I did and she's coming.

Karen Oh, Freya! You didn't. Where is she?

Freya Quite near.

Karen We're going. (*She gathers up her things*)

Ruth and Matt enter

Matt Come on, love, everyone's leaving now. She's feeling a bit better. Did you have your brandy?

Ruth Yes, with a Valium.

Freya (*giving Ruth a hug*) I think Ruth's been like, totally brilliant.

Ruth Thank you Freya. I'm sorry about before. I shouldn't have said all that. It's just been, a bit, much.

Matt Hey, I think you're brilliant, too.

Ruth And I think maybe it's time we all —— (*she indicates the door*)

Karen Absolutely. Come on Freya. Quickly, before ——

The doorbell rings

Oh no!

Ruth (*sighing*) Who the heck's that now? Maybe it's another child Matt forgot to tell us about.

Freya It'll be Bev.

Ruth Bev?

Freya I hope you don't mind?

Ruth No. Why should I? Bev, Bev's friend, her friend's sister. Why don't we just put Open House on the door?

The bell rings again

Karen You had no business asking that woman ——

Freya She's my auntie

Karen She is not your auntie. She's a troublemake ——

Freya — You may not like her, but I do. She's always nice to me.

Karen That's because she doesn't have to live with you.

The bell rings again

Ruth Come in, Bev, whoever you are. Join the happy throng. Any time of day or night.

Matt Shall I? (*He shrugs*) I'd better. (*He opens the front door*)

Bev is standing at the door

Hello.

Bev Hiya! You must be Matt, eh? (*Barging in*) Is our Freya here?

Freya Auntie Bev!

Bev Hiya, babe, don't you look great? Hello, Karen. Well, aren't you going to introduce me?

Freya This is Auntie Bev.

Karen She had no business. We're going.

Bev What d'you mean? I've only just got here.

Freya Oh, Mum, she's come specially.

Ruth Would somebody care to explain?

Freya It was Bev who like, helped me, to trace Matt?

Matt pours a glass of wine. Pauline sits, bag on knee, determined not to miss anything

Bev I made her promise she'd let me know. And she did, bless her. (*To Ruth*) I hope you don't mind, love.

Ruth Who am I to mind?

Bev Oh good. Let's see then. So you're Dad are you? Very nice. And this must be Grandma. Hello Grandma. (*To Ruth*) And you must be ——

Ruth I am no one, Bev. I just live here. And there was me thinking my life was empty, lacked meaning. Lacked children. And all I had to look forward to was another boring evening with my husband when all of a sudden, surprise, surprise, I find out he's got a whole new beautiful family. And here they all are, lovely daughter, Mummy, Daddy, Granny, now we've got Auntie. All here in our little flat. Well, aren't I the lucky one. Yes, siree. So, make yourselves at home. Have some nuts, some crisps, what about some Valium? No? Have another drink then. Come on, Matt, make them at home. Crisps, drinks, burned lasagne?

Somewhat alarmed by this outburst but anxious to please, Matt offers the company the wine glass he's filled

Matt Anyone?

The others all ignore him. He drains the glass and pours himself another

Bev So, Ruth. It is Ruth? You didn't know anything about this?
Ruth Nothing whatsoever.
Matt I didn't, either.
Ruth So, Bev. It is Bev? How do you fit into this saga?
Bev I'm a very important part of it ——
Karen We have to go, please, now.
Freya Ah, Mum —— !
Ruth No, Karen, let's not spoil a wonderful evening. As Bev said, she's only just got here, and we mustn't disappoint little Freya must we? Mustn't ever do that. So where does Bev come in?
Bev Well, Freya rang me up last year, didn't you, honey? You know, wanting help with tracking down her dad. I know you weren't keen, Karen, but she *was* eighteen and entitled to know. I presume you've told her *all* of it. Where I came in, and all that?
Karen I don't feel very well ——
Freya Told me about what?
Karen Please, Bev!
Bev It's nothing to be ashamed of, Karen.

Karen's knees buckle dramatically

Ruth Oh, catch her. Sit her here. Matt! Drink of water.

Matt exits to the kitchen

Now. Get her head between her knees. Her colour's very good, for a faint.

Matt returns with a glass of water and hands it to Ruth

Take a sip of this. All right Karen?
Karen Not really. (*To Freya*) I want to go home. Call Robin.
Freya Not yet, that's so unfair. (*To Bev*) What did you mean, like, "have you told her?"
Karen That's enough!
Freya Told me what?
Bev How you were born, love.

Karen La, la la la ——

Ruth Is there something else?

Bev Not half there is. I thought you'd told her.

Freya Told me what?

Karen (*shouting*) Don't!

Bev It's nothing to be ashamed of — you see, your mam couldn't ——

Freya — get pregnant with my dad — the one I used to call Dad, I know that.

Bev She couldn't get pregnant at all, love, that's where I came in.

Ruth What are you saying?

Bev She had the eggs, but they wouldn't take. And there was me, five kids in five years, like shelling peas, I take, just like that, and I loved being pregnant — it was the babies I wasn't so fussed on. You know, once they can answer back you go off them. So there's her with the eggs, all homeless like, and me with the womb ——

Matt Offering vacancies.

Bev That's right.

Matt Wombs to let.

Ruth Matt! (*To Bev*) Are you saying —— ?

Freya What?

Ruth You gave birth to Freya?

Bev Certainly did.

Freya So what does —— ? Ohmygod, is she my mother?

Karen No, Freya! I am your mother. She promised not to interfere in any way.

Bev And nor have I, Karen. Except for birthdays. I always sent her a card, didn't I, love? And a little prezzy from Auntie Bev. That's not interference is it?

Karen It most certainly is. You promised, Bev!

Freya This is so, like unbelievable?

Pauline Well you've got me completely lost now.

The doorbell rings

Ruth Oh, now there's somebody else. Why not? Let's have a bloody street party. (*She opens the front door*)

Robin, a butch-looking woman, is standing at the door

Yes?

Robin I've come to pick up Karen and Freya.

Ruth Thank goodness. There's a taxi here for you, Karen.

Robin God, no, I'm not a taxi. I'm Robin. (*She barges in, past Ruth*)

Ruth stands bewildered at the door

Oh, quite a crowd. I didn't realise.

Ruth You're not the only one.

Robin Karen, there you are. You've been ages, so I thought I'd best call. How did it go?

Karen Indescribable.

Ruth I'd second that.

Freya It's been amazing. Totally amazing.

Robin There you are, kid, I knew it would be. So, who's who?

Freya Well, first, this is my, like, Dad!

Robin Hi, Dad. (*Slapping his arm*) Hey, pretty cool, eh? I'm Robin.

Bev Oh. So *you're* Robin? Well, well.

Robin What's it to you? Well, introduce me, Freya. Who's this?

Freya This is my new Gran!

Robin Oh, hi, Gran! Been a bit of a surprise, eh?

Pauline That's an understatement

Robin And who's that over by the door?

Ruth (*still holding the door*) Just ignore me, I'm no one.

Robin Ah never mind. Why don't you come in and get yourself warm? It's freezing out there.

Ruth I think I might just go, actually, leave you all to sort it out.

Karen No, *we're* going.

Robin Hey, not yet, love. I've only just got here.

Ruth Funny, they've all said that. And here they all are, still.

Bev It's a good job I came, if you ask me.

Robin Who's she?

Freya This is Bev.

Robin Oh, the famous Bev, you've turned up have you?

Bev Not that it's any of your business.

Robin Listen, you, anything that affects Karen *is* my business. So what you doing here? Come to cause trouble?

Bev What are *you* doing here, more like? Poor little Freya. Sick, I call it.

Robin Hah, you make *me* sick. Why couldn't you have stayed away?

Bev I've more right here than you have.

Robin Oh no you have not.

Matt Excuse me, d'you mind me asking, who are you?

Robin Who am I? I'm Karen's partner, who d'you think? Five years now, isn't it, darling?

Karen *(quietly)* That's right.

Ruth closes the door slowly

Pauline Are they in business together, then?

Bev Not the sort of business you'd approve of.

Matt I thought Karen had a husband?

Robin Oh yes, she did once, but then she saw the light. All men are rapists you know.

Bev Oh for God's sake.

Matt Well I'm certainly not. And wasn't. There was no intimate contact. No contact at all actually.

Ruth An "Immaculate Conception."

Robin Best way if you ask me. Karen and me were thinking of trying for another one, actually.

Freya No way!

Matt Well, don't be looking at me.

Ruth So much for Karen fancying you.

Freya Oh, she probably does. My mother's got like, confused sexuality?

Bev Poor babe, it gets worse.

Freya No, it's really cool, to have two gay parents.

Robin Yes. So I've applied to adopt her.

Freya I don't think so.

Bev That's disgusting.

Robin It's you that's disgusting.

A pause

Pauline Would someone mind telling me what the heck's going on?

Ruth Sorry about all this, Pauline. It wasn't planned, I assure you.

Pauline What I don't understand is how could *she* adopt Freya? That'd be two mothers.

Freya And I've already got two, with you and Bev.

Karen No you haven't ——

Bev Yes you have, I'm your tummy mummy.

Robin Oh for God's sake.

Freya So that'd make three. Tummy Mummy ——

Robin Karen's Yummy Mummy, and I'd be ——

Bev Scummy Mummy.

Robin Ha ha... cow.

Bev Pervert.

Karen Stop it! Please.

Freya This is really wicked. That's three mothers. And Ruth, you're like a stepmother, that makes four!

Ruth Oh no, leave me out.

Freya Ohmygod, four mothers, that is so bizarre.

Matt Bizarre, it's bloody mad.

Karen How could you, Bev? You promised.

Bev Well you shouldn't have cut me off like that. You never considered my feelings, did you? When I held her, that first time ——

Karen You weren't supposed to hold her. It was all agreed. You were to hand her over.

Robin That's right. Just hand her over.

Bev Mind your own business, you weren't even there.

Robin Oh shut your face.

Freya I so don't believe this. "Hand her over?" Like I was a chicken, in Sainsburys?

Bev I carried her for nine months. She was part of me. Six hours in labour, and you didn't even want me to hold her.

Karen Well that was the agreement.

Robin A deal's a deal if you ask me.

Bev Nobody asked you, and anyway, what would someone like you know about having babies?

Robin What d'you mean, like me?

Bev I'd have thought it obvious. *(To Freya)* Honestly, love, you've been reunited with your real mum, then there's all this unpleasantness ——

Robin You are *not* her mother. We are.

Freya I so don't want to be adopted. No way.

Bev There you are!

Robin Mind your own business, you nasty, interfering cow.

Bev Mind yours, you stupid, interfering pervert.

Robin What! What did you say? Come here, you nasty ——

Robin grabs Bev's hair. Bev fights back. Matt and Karen intervene and manage to separate them

Matt Hey, ladies, come on! No need for that!

Karen Don't, Robin, she's not worth it.

Robin Don't you ever call me that, you ——

Karen — Leave it. Just ignore her. Come on, love.

Robin *(shouting)* Sexual discrimination that is. It's illegal you know. I'll report you. I will. You're all witnesses.

Bev Go ahead, see if I care.

Ruth Have you quite finished?

Karen Oh, this is a nightmare. I'm so sorry.

Freya Don't get upset, Mum.

Robin None of it's your fault, hon.

Karen Well whose fault is it? If I hadn't gone to that clinic ——

Matt If *I* hadn't gone to that clinic ——

Robin If *she* hadn't left well alone —— *(indicating Bev)*

Freya If *I* hadn't let well alone. I don't know ——

Ruth There's a good rule, Freya, if you're not certain you'll like the answer, best not to ask the question.

Robin I quite agree. I'm going to wait in the car. *(To Karen)* Don't be long, love. Bye all. *(Leaving. To Bev)* Bye, bitch.

Bev Bye, cow.

Robin exits

Ruth (*sighing heavily*) Are you all right, Pauline?

Pauline I only came over to bring a crumble.

Ruth I know. Poor you.

Pauline Poor you.

Freya This is so doing my head in. So who is like, really my mother? The egg one, or the womb one?

Pauline Well I'm totally confused.

Ruth (*kindly, to Karen*) The one who brought you up of course.

Karen Who went through the teething, sleepless nights. Putting up with your tantrums. Loving you. No matter what.

Ruth Doing whatever you asked. Like all this. I hope you're happy, Freya.

Freya This is so not my fault.

Ruth Huh!

Freya I never asked to be born.

Ruth No. But I bet you're glad you were.

Pauline There was none of this nonsense in my day.

Ruth They call it progress, Pauline. A right to this, a right to that. I see it at work all the time. Matt and I even considered IVF ourselves at one time. But people don't think. You're hurt, Freya, I'm hurt, and Matt.

Matt The father you rejected? Bet he was hurt.

Ruth And your Mum, Freya. She was only doing her best.

Pauline It's been a shock for me, you know.

Matt Oh for heaven's sake, Mother. If it wasn't for your interference you'd have been none the wiser.

Ruth That's not fair, Matt.

Pauline All I was doing was bringing you food. I won't bother again.

Matt We're doing fine, thank you. And Ruth is a fantastic wife, who puts up with me, and I hope she still will.

Ruth Of course I will.

Bev Don't mind me, will you?

Matt What do you expect? What *did* you expect?

Freya (*to Bev*) Did you get money for doing that?

Karen Oh yes, she did. A lot actually

Freya Paid for using your body? That is so gross. Like a prostitute.

Bev You try to help people ——

Ruth By coming here, who have you helped?

Bev She had a right to know. And I've got rights as well.

Ruth That's what everyone says these days. Well, I think it was spiteful.

Freya So do I.

Bev I see. Right, I'll go then. That's the thanks you get.

Ruth opens the front door

Goodbye, Freya.

Bev exits

Freya Bye, Auntie Bev.

Ruth shrugs, then shuts the door

Karen (*to Freya*) You knew how I felt about Bev.

Freya But not "why".

Ruth And that's all that mattered to you.

Freya I can't believe you went through all that.

Karen I was desperate for a child.

Freya You'd do, like, anything?

Ruth Yes. So don't you be hard on her. I know. You would do anything. (*Pause*) She goes through all that. Years of care, sacrifices, and what happens? She ends up with an ungrateful little madam like you.

Matt Ruth!

Freya That is so out of order.

Karen Ruth's tired.

Pauline I'm not surprised. All this.

Freya I am *so* not ungrateful.

Karen Well that's something.

Freya This is all, totally, amazing? All my friends were just, like, *born*. That's so, like, *boring*. Did you really want me, that much?

Karen Of course I did.

Freya Oh Mum. You are so, like, totally, brilliant. Mmm, love you, love you.

Karen And I love you.

Pauline Ah, isn't that nice. (*To Ruth*) I didn't know you'd been trying.

Ruth Pauline, if you only knew.

Matt comforts Ruth

Pauline We started a lot younger in our day, didn't have all this trouble. I wonder what the world's coming to. Look at the time. I'd best be off, Will you call me a taxi?

Matt Right away. Then there's something else I want to do.

Matt makes a call then works at his computer during the following dialogue

Freya fiddles with her mobile

Pauline Well. Freya, Granny has to be off. OK, love?

Freya continues to concentrate on her phone

Bye, Freya love. Your Granny's going!

Freya Oh shit, my battery's running out.

Pauline (*perplexed*) I don't know. It is another world.

Ruth I'm sorry about, all this, Pauline.

Pauline It's worse for you, I reckon. And you've got work tomorrow. What time do you start?

Ruth Six thirty

Pauline Not right you having to do those hours. That lad of mine wants to get a proper job. Look after yourself, eh? I'll wait outside, it's stopped raining.

Ruth I'll wait with you, I could do with the air.

Pauline Bye, love!

Karen Goodbye … Freya!

Freya Oh yes, bye. Ohmygod, it's completely dead!

Pauline and Ruth exchange rueful smiles and exit

Matt, please, please, can I use your phone? I am so, like, stressed. Martine said she'd phone — and if she's texted, my battery's down. I so need to call her? Please Daddy?

Matt shrugs and hands over the phone. Freya dials

Karen Freya! Make it quick. Matt I'm sorry about everything. I feel really ——
Matt Don't mention it. Would you mind if I just finish ——
Karen Of course, sorry.

Matt continues at the keyboard during the following, then eventually turns off the computer

There is the sound of a taxi arriving and Pauline leaving

Ruth comes back in

Freya (*into the phone*) I'm actually on their phone now? And yeah, they're really cool? … Tonight? Who's coming? Jamie! Ohmygod! I so am coming. What you wearing? … The one from Topshop? I so wanted that top. Can I borrow your red halter? Please, please, kiss kiss … About an hour I think. Mum'll bring me straight to yours, get changed, then Jamie here I come! Can't wait! Bye, see ya soon. (*She turns the phone off. Then, wheedling*) Mum?
Karen The answer is no!
Freya Ah, Mum, please … Love you!
Karen No. *You* wanted to come here. We've had nothing else for the past ——
Freya But Jamie'll be there. Please, please!
Karen I said no.
Freya (*furious*) You are so unfair. I said I'd go and I'm going.

Karen Not this time, no.

Freya You never let me do anything. I hate you, I really really hate you.

Matt Hey, Freya, you shouldn't talk to your mum like that.

Freya Mind your own business, you're not my father. So stuff you as well.

Matt Oh I see.

Karen We'd better go. I'm really sorry about this.

Freya (*heading for the door, happy again*) We can be there by eleven if we go now.

Karen I'll call you, Ruth.

Ruth Fine. No hurry. (*Calling*) Freya? Just one little thing.

Freya What?

Ruth This Jamie, if you're really keen on him, you'd better have his DNA checked.

Freya Why?

Ruth Well, he could be your brother, you never know.

Freya That is so gross.

Ruth Just a thought.

Freya Mum! Let's go, I'll be late.

Karen Don't be so rude. Say goodbye to Ruth and Matt. And there'll be no party.

Furious, Freya stomps out of the house

Ruth ⎫
Matt ⎬ (*together*) Goodbye, Freya!

Ruth and Matt shrug wryly at the lack of response

Karen Freya!

Freya (*off, calling*) I *am* going. You can't stop me. Come *on*!

Karen I wonder if Bev still wants her?

Freya (*off, yelling*) Mum!

Karen Bye, thanks for everything.

Karen hurries out

Ruth shuts the door

Ruth Any time! Not.
Matt Not, not, not, not, not… (*trailing off*)

They collapse onto the sofa with groans of relief

Matt Have you ever wished you could start a day all over again?
Ruth Absolutely. And to think we thought we wanted kids.
Matt Narrow escape, eh?
Ruth Not half. (*Pause*) Wow.
Matt Wow.
Ruth Matt?
Matt Mm?
Ruth When you met Freya, did you feel anything? You know, any sense of, connection? Anything?
Matt No. Just a great sense of relief now she's gone. No, no bond, no feeling at all. No. Just shows you. (*Pause*) Just thinking, it's a great plot.
Ruth What? For the Pulitzer novel?
Matt That's right. "Rogue Gene" I could call it. It would be *this* story, more or less. But years later, *dozens* of kids start turning up — all created from the same batch.
Ruth Dozens of them? Imagine! No, don't! So what's next?
Matt Then Karl — he's the hero.
Ruth Of course.
Matt He finds out he's got this gene, that's been passed on to all of them ——
Ruth And what does it do?
Matt I haven't quite decided yet.
Ruth How about it makes them spontaneously combust when they reach their teens!

Ruth and Matt laugh

Matt Perfect. You can share the movie rights.

Ruth and Matt sit quietly, lost in thought

Ruth I keep thinking someone else'll come barging through the door.

Matt I know. What an evening.

Ruth Matt. There's nothing else you need to tell me, is there? Now's the time.

Matt Well yes, actually.

Ruth Oh Matt. What?

Matt I've booked a weekend in Venice.

Ruth Honestly? Oh that's fantastic. (*Pause*) I am invited?

Matt What do you think?

Ruth Thank you. And just the two of us?

Matt Oh yes. Just the two of us.

Ruth Do you know something, Matt?

Matt What?

Ruth You're just like, *so, totally*, brilliant.

Matt And you're like, *so, totally*, wicked!

Ruth Am I? (*She kisses him*)

Matt Mm! D'you know, now I'm feeling a bit wicked, so — what about bed?

Ruth Sounds good to me. (*She rises*)

Matt You get ready.

Ruth I am so tired. You'd best not be long. (*Exiting*) You will check that door's locked?

Matt I certainly will. Locked, bolted and barricaded — you bet your sweet life.

Black-out

FURNITURE AND PROPERTY LIST

On stage: Sofa
Small table. *On it*: Tray set for simple supper for two; wine
    glasses
Chairs
Desk. *On it*: phone, computer, printer
Desk chair
Bin

Offstage: Mug of tea (**Matt**)
Wine bottle (**Matt**)
Bag (**Karen**)
Two glasses (**Matt**)
Blackened, smoking pan (**Matt**)
Pudding dish wrapped in tea towel, carrier bag containing
cream, custard and photograph wallet (**Pauline**)
Two packets of crisps (**Freya**)
Glass of water (**Matt**)

Personal: **Freya**: mobile phone

LIGHTING PLOT

Practical fittings required: nil

S<small>CENE</small> 1

To open: General interior lighting

Cue 1: **Freya**: "Come and meet Granny!"   (Page 19)
          Black-out

S<small>CENE</small> 2

To open: General interior lighting

Cue 2: **Matt**: "You bet your sweet life."   (Page 38)
          Black-out

EFFECTS PLOT

Printed by The Kingfisher Press, London NW10 7AS